BLUE
MARROW

BLUE MARROW

LOUISE • BERNICE • HALFE

COTEAU BOOKS
WWW.COTEAUBOOKS.COM

Edited by Tim Lilburn
Cover and book design by Duncan Campbell
Cover images: the author's grandmothers, and "Northern Lights," Digital Vision / Veer
Cover montage by Duncan Campbell
Printed and bound in Canada at Gauvin Press

Library and Archives Canada Cataloguing in Publication

Halfe, Louise Bernice, 1953-
Blue marrow / Louise Bernice Halfe.

Poems.
Previously published: Toronto : M&S, 1998.
Includes some text in Cree.
1sbn: 978-1-55050-304-3

1. Cree Indians—Poetry. I. Title.

ps8565.a4335b558 2004   c811'.54   c2004-904964-x

Short Run July 2015

2517 Victoria Avenue
Regina, Saskatchewan
Canada S4P 0T2
www.coteaubooks.com

Available in Canada from:
Publishers Group Canada
2440 Viking Way
Richmond, British Columbia
Canada V6V 1N2

Coteau Books gratefully acknowledges the financial support of its publishing program by: the Saskatchewan Arts Board, the Canada Council for the Arts, the Government of Canada through the Canada Book Fund, the Government of Saskatchewan through the Creative Economy Entrepreneurial Fund, the Association for the Export of Canadian Books and the City of Regina Arts Commission.

Blue Marrow *is dedicated to*
nikâwiy – *Madeleine Waskewidch*
and nôhkom – *Adeline Half.*

Voice Dancer *pawâkan,* the Guardian of Dreams and Visions, prayer, brings to you this gift.

> *Glory be to* okâwîmâwaskiy
> *To the* nôhkom âtayôhkan
> *To* pawâkan
> *As it was in the Beginning,*
> *Is now,*
> *And ever shall be,*
> *World without end.*
> *Amen. Amen.*

The walk began before I was a seed.

My mother strung my umbilical cord in my moccasins.

When I was a grasshopper *nimosôm* would open a big book. His fingers traced the path of *cahkipêhikana* / ⊲̇ ᒷ △ ·ᐤ, mouth moving quietly.

Long after *nimosôm* died my memory went to sleep. I woke in the mountains lying in the crook of my white husband's arms, cocooned in the warmth of our teepee.

nimosôm took my fingers and guided me through his book. Another old man sat in the grove of trees, lifted his Pipe, my hands on the stem.

When I returned to the cabin I filled the pockets between the logs with papers, stacked the walls with my books. A man, braids hanging past his shoulders, laughed.

Still in my walks, the mountains beneath my feet, I picked feathers as I climbed, the wolves gentle in their following. Soon the mountain too had feet. I swam down her clear water and stood naked beneath her falls.

Nearby, windburned fences enclosed crosses, their hinged grey arms dangled. I heard screams and gunshot in the early dawn. After the fierce weeping of thunder and mad dash of lightning, the robins danced with the drumming of the Little People. I woke as the brilliant ribbon of Northern Lights melted into a sunrise.

I was stuck, the weasel untangled my braids, ran down my heart while *nôhkom* sat at the foot of the bed, her weight shifting as she sang. I walked up the mountain again, loaded with gifts.

âstam, she said. She rubbed my eyes with her sweat and I saw her many faces.

Each face sat at the altar with one large eye.

We picked chokecherries, lips stained. Crushed them between the rocks.

In her cabin where *nôhkom* waited was a stoneboat stacked full of her belongings. Spotted blue enamel plates, oversize spoons, crazy quilts. She invited all my relatives to her feast.

She sang, her Voices echoing through the cabin. As I slept through the songs my hands became rocks too heavy to lift. Ants scurried in and out of the cracks, carrying crumbs, chewing bits of dirt, digging many holes. Eggs squirmed.

I'm awake now and remove my ring.

When I married him I dragged the cord past the road where my reserve ended.

ê-kî-âhtaskêyân, they said. I put my land elsewhere when I became his wife.

The prairie is full of bones. The bones stand and sing and I feel the weight of them as they guide my fingers on this page.

2

See the blood.

On my left breast was a hoofprint. It disappeared when I began the walk for them:

> okâwîmâwaskiy
> *full of grace;*
> *The Creator is filled with thee;*
> *Blessed art thou among* iskwêwak
> *and blessed is the fruit of thy womb,*
> *Holy Mother of all*
> *Pray for us* kitânisak,
> *now and at the hour*
> *of our death. Amen.*

Adeline Cardinal. Emma Woods. Sara Cardinal. Bella Shirt. Nancy Gladue. Fanny Sunchild. Round Face Woman. Charlotte. Ah-gat. Bernard Woman. Pray to them.

> *Glory be to* okâwîmâwaskiy
> *And to* nôhkom âtayôhkan

wâpâsôs – Up At Dawn Woman. Frying Pan Woman. Vera. Pauline Johnson. Shawnidit. Waskedich Woman. Wet Pants Woman. Carter Woman. Rubber Mouth Woman. Louiza. Ehnah – Sarcee Woman. Pray to them.

> *And to* pawâkan
> *As it was in the beginning.*

Lightning Woman. McGuiness Woman. One Spot Woman. Campbell Woman. Benson Woman. Sun Dog Woman. Rainy Bird Woman. Windy Boy Woman. Small Woman. Stump Woman. Pray to them.

Is now,
And ever shall be

Boudreau Woman. Lizzbeth. Large Woman. Rocky Boy Woman.
Cameron Woman. Clearwater Woman. Cuthand Woman. Good
Leaf Woman. Kingfisher Woman. Lameman Woman. Pray to
them.

World without end.
Amen. Amen.

Linklater Woman. Morin Woman. Many Fingers Woman. Martin
Woman. Minnie. Moosewah Woman. Kathleen. Pasqua Woman.
Shirt Woman. Carlson Woman. Pray to them.

okâwîmâwaskiy
who art in tawahikan
Hallowed be thy name

McGilvery Woman. Fiddler Woman. Cook Woman. Horse Dance
Woman. Russell Woman. Whitecloud Woman. Snake Woman. She
Flies Strong and Swift Woman. Yellow Knee Woman. Swiftwolf
Woman. Pray to them.

Thy Creation come
Thy will be done

Sitting Weasel Woman. She Has Strong Back Strong Wings
Woman. Bosivert Woman. Thompson's Mistress. Jobson Woman.
Factor Grant's Woman. Desjarlais Woman. Ross Woman. Kewin
Woman. Bear Woman. Pray to them.

asiskiy *as it is in* kîsik
Give us this day our daily reminders

Hamelin Woman. Wailing Woman. Sky Woman. Littlestick
Woman. *wâpawês* Woman. Black's Woman. Connolly Woman.
Dodging Horse Woman. Suzanne. Flora. Pray to them.

of sâkihitowin, *of* kisêwâtisiwin
And forgive us our shortcomings
As we forgive those who trespass against us

Big Heels Woman. Little Bear Woman. Night Traveller Woman.
cicîmân Woman. Trottier Woman. Ugly Face Woman. Little
Hunter Woman. Lone Woman. Crooked Neck Woman. Ballenden
Woman. Pray to them.

Oh mâmaw-ôhtâwîmâw
Lead us into Celebration

Buffalo Woman. Bear Hat Woman. Eliza. Mouse Woman.
Whistling Eagle Woman. Blackman Woman. Berland Woman.
McNeil Woman. *wâsatinaw* Woman. Quintal Woman. Pray to
them.

We give you thanks for the Four Legged.
The Winged People. The Swimmers.

Whiskyjack Woman. Rabbit Woman. Pond Woman. Blackfeather
Woman. Memnook Woman. Ironman Woman. Fur-Trader's Wife.
First Wife Woman. Bone Woman. Thunder Woman. Pray to
them.

We give thanks to the piyêsiwak –
Whose voice sings from kîsik.

Callihoo Woman. A Bunch of Bitches Woman. Rolling Head
Woman – *cihcipistikwân*. Striped Gopher Woman. Wildman
Woman. Little Chief Woman. Badger Woman. Horse Woman.
Watchmaker Woman. Silver Cloud Woman. Pray to them.

We give thanks to the nôtokwêsiwak
We give thanks to the kisêyiniwak
The Keeper of the âcimowinis
nôhkom âtayôhkan

Sparkling Eyes Woman. Ermineskin Woman. Littlechild Woman.
Janvier Woman. Giant Woman. Youngchief Woman. Oaks
Woman. Squirrel Net Woman. Macleod *iskwêw.* Simpson's
Woman. Pray to them.

mâmaw-ôhtâwîmâw,
who art in tawahikan
Hallowed be thy name

McDougall Woman. Douglas Woman. McTavish Woman.
Matooskiie. Fraser Woman. Batoche Woman. Big Plume Woman.
Melting Tallow Woman. Big Stone Woman. Thanadelthur
Woman. Pray to them.

Lead us to Creation and
Deliver us into mâmitonêyihtêstamâsowin
into the matotisân

Bright Eyes Woman. Wander Spirit Woman. Damn You Woman.
Lip Pointing Woman. Baptiste Woman. Thunder Child Woman.
Sonnabitch Woman. Tallman Woman. Sky Dance Woman.
Crowfoot Woman. Pray to them.

For thou art the Parent of All, the connection,
and the Centre, the Universe
the power

Cardinal Woman. Mud Hen Woman. Old Woman. Fire Thunder
Woman. Kicking Horse Woman. Big Swan Woman. *kâ-itwêhât –*
She Who Says So Woman. To all *nîci* Women. All my Relations.
Amen.

the glory
Now and for ever
Amen. Amen.

Grandmothers hold me.
I must pass all that I possess,
every morsel to my children.
These small gifts.

These crumbs of memory serve me with deep affection and fear. *nôhkomak*, the four of them. How well I remember them. Adeline, my father's mother. Huge, forbearing medicine woman. One day she wanted to visit across the road, my cousin and I loaded her in the sleigh and off we went, my cousin and I huffing and puffing, each of us trying to ease our load by stealing the slack off the rope, *nôhkom* pretending we were her horses. My cousin and I conspiring. Oh yes, we let her race down that hill, flopping and bouncing, screeching and swearing as that toboggan flew. We held our sides as we walked quietly behind her. After she died she'd visit me along with my other *nôhkomak*. Stirring the dirt altar, silent and deep.

nôhkom Emma. She always arrived late in the evening, climbing the small hill, swinging her cane. And if she wasn't walking she galloped sidesaddle stirring the dust behind her. She must've been married to a white man, 'cause my cousins they all have that white skin. Guess you can say that about my father too, white-skinned Indian, though *nimosôm* and Adeline were Indian, as Indian as me anyway. Where else would *nôhkom* Emma learn to ride English? But *nôhkom* Emma, there was nothing white woman about her. She picked her medicine riding, walking house to house. She was our minstrel woman, travelling poet of her time. Maybe it's she who sings through these fingers. She was there too, kind old wise woman sitting with *nôhkom* Adeline, in front of that altar.

nôhkom Bella, she's the one who loved to laugh. I wish I knew her better. One night many nights ago a man from away on horseback snatched *nôhkom* Bella as she lay beneath the stars dreaming. *nôhkom* flapped her arms and legs so hard she socked her Blackfoot captor. She went flying to *nimosôm*'s horse. Since that day *nimosôm* kept her behind the "scream door," she said, swaggering. *nôhkom* Bella was a hen with babies beneath her wings. She carried jokes in her belly. Waddling and clucking. She lived on the other side of the hill from *nôhkom* Adeline. I think they sent messages in the air, each sitting on their beds, huge-like cooking, brewing medicine. *nôhkom* Bella, her fingers warm on my cheek, making room for me at the altar.

And then *nôhkom* Sarah. Everyone called her Sayna. Sayna, she was a midwife, delivered many babies on the reserve. She had a tongue. Knife, scissors cutting the air with the sureness of babies ripping, bellowing like small buffalo. Oh yes, this *nôhkom* you didn't mess with. Yet she always had that wonderful rabbit, hot and perking, bannock melting in your mouth. Her herbs stick into me bitter like ratroot, sweet like wild carrot, make my mouth water all at once. I burn from her brilliant stare. She sits there on the altar with the rest of them.

> Oh Sarah, Adeline,
> Oh Emma, Bella,
> tongueless in the earth.
> Oh *nôhkomak,*
> your Bundles I carry inside,
> the full moon dancing
> beyond my wails.
> I've seeped into
> your faces,
> drowned in the pictures
> I have gathered
> and
> cannot
> hold.

I sit by the window
Thick woodsmoke lets the moon shine in.
I take my finger and walk it,
leave mice-size tracks.
The cabin is warm with the smell of bannock.
This long bone I hold
leaves me calloused and cold.
A few months ago I chewed all the meat
and now I've become clever.
I press these words hard
with charcoal
over and over
so I can write.
The little ones with dirty blond hair
look at me with dawn's eyes. I travel with them
into their backyard
where those men of god docked their ships,
took brown wives,
left them in barns and stalls –
horseflies and mosquitoes.
Many years have passed.
The moon our only eye,
it travels the silent roar of the lake,
the grand stillness of the rocks.
These blond children of the fur traders
seep through our women
even though they have long remarried
into the dark bark of our grain.
Their grandmother's chant cuts
the air on a dead drum,
"devil's spawn, devil's spawn."
Over the hills the bone climbs
slowly past the metal crosses
pounded in the ditches,
nailed hubcaps shine
in the centre of the holy bones.

Every dirt car rattling over this washboard road,
its braided passengers crossing themselves.
The sign of the cross is never holy.

A little red rose and lonesome charlie
spilled through the mud-stained windows
slur jesus' name.
They pass where someone saw
mary's radiance.
I see her myself, radiant, her bloody hands,
her bloody heart, her half-starved face.
She draws
till my head is a massive throb.

I am in this room.

A mosquito buzzes my arm.
I've smudged with sage.
I think repelling thought
for the mosquito and these icons.
My hunt is without a rifle,
without a net,
my bone
filled with the fists of women
of the fur trade.

The orange sunset dies
beneath broken beer bottles,
the birds cackle
in the embers of the dying heat.

I receive a rock in the mail.
Hummingbird sends a wing.
I barricade myself.
My fingers crows,

ravens the computer.
Quebec. Referendum.
I sip *okinîwâpoy.*
Chew *wîhkês.*
Notes slip under my door.
I can hardly get past my throat.

Large white splattering
at the House.
Feathered people storming.

Columbus wrote:
"My wound has opened again."

His bones at the cathedral of Santa Domingo
moved four times,
different burial grounds.
In the last move his ashes
spill and are trampled.

Possession took me last night.
I slept with a bone.
The jawbone of elk lined with pearly teeth.
I bathed her in sweet grass. Laid her under my pillow.
Winds swept through me. This path has chosen me,
this chosen walk is a blizzard whiteout.
My Cree-ing alone in the heavy arm of snow.

I hang onto this bone
dressed in satin. Wade into redberry lakes.
I am married
to her garden of carrots and sweet corn heads.
I lay her skull, broken jaws,
face them to the East.

When *nôhkom*'s granddaughter slept
on top of graves
I thought she was crazy. All night I danced
above her head.
She dragged a string of skulls, heavy
in torrent rains. Cree-ing loud into my night.

I sleep with rocks too.
I couldn't say this before.
Who could I say it to except *nôhkom*'s granddaughter?
The rocks fill me. Their stories,
slates in dreams, heavy in my stomach,
move like thick clouds blown by my laboured breathing.
I cannot catch them.
I don't think to ask them
to slow down.

I sleep with petrified wood too.
Frozen snails, snakes with amber eyes,
crystallized tails.

Soon the black robes
will burn me,
stake me to their cross.
I won't have to live
in whiteouts much longer.

pê-nîhtaciwêk, nôhkomak.
pê-nânapâcihinân.
kwâhkotêw, nipônênân.
pê-nîhtaciwêk, nôhkomak.
pê-nânapâcihinân.
ê-sôhkêpayik. kimaskihkîm.
kâ-wî-nânapâcihikoyâhk.

pê-nîhtaciwêk, nôhkomak.
kitimâkinawinân. sawêyiminân.

pê-nîhtaciwêk, nôhkomak.
Climb down, my Grandmothers.

pê-nânapâcihinân.
Come heal us.

The thick fog, the fog has lifted.
The ice shattered.

The crossing of the roads
is where we wait.

pê-nîhtaciwêk, nôhkomak.
Climb down, my Grandmothers.

pê-nânapâcihinân.
Come heal us.

ê-sôhkêpayik. kimaskihkîm.
Your medicine so powerful.

kâ-wî-nânapâcihikoyâhk.
That which will heal us.

pê-nîhtaciwêk, nôhkomak.
Climb down, my Grandmothers.

kitimâkinawinân. sawêyiminân.
Take pity on us. Bless us.

Bless me, father. I've pierced my flesh. Danced
with the Sun. Bathed my face in blood.
I didn't mean to.
Forgive me, father. I ask for absolution.
I promise to say my rosary and serve my time.
I promise to keep my hands to myself and
swallow my tongue. Amen.

We gathered in the darkened room,
bodies pressed leg to leg. Our breath
mint and garlic, sage and sweet grass
woven into my burlap gown.
We held hands, my love and I.
On each side my mother and father sat.
Blankets tea sugar flour gunpowder.
Tobacco ribbon blueberry cloth.
In the dark they came.

I bring to you
these Voices I will not name. Voices
filled with bird calls, snorting buffalo,
kicking bears, mountain goats.
I do not recognize who speaks.
Skin unfolds. Sag after sag.
Words squeezed through her
blistered tongues
lick till my heart stings, my
eyes swell.

Lightning flitted.
Scorched our flesh.
They tore out our tongues.
When we spoke,
my love and I, darkness swelled.
Thunder became our footsteps. This
ceremonial dance of my dead.
We were wedded that night.
The night has no shadow,
her veil always an open mouth.
Listen to the bones.

ohkomipan, *I am she who speaks, father, the Eternal*
Grandmother.
Forgive me father, for I have sinned. It has been since
1492 since my last confession. I have committed the
following sins.

Ripped my robes. Thrown into sea.
Spirit on their soil.

They tore flesh, breasts became pouches, hung
from their belts. Our bellies spilled.
I hung myself.

Blankets kill us. I am a large scab.

Mass graves. Fingers dig still
through the many bones.

Burned our crops. We live on mice.
We hold a Begging Dance.
Still our bellies echo.

Shot our babies, crushed their skulls against the rocks
The great mother sends more gods
to sprinkle water
on our heads.

The land weeps. I am choking. Choking.
The buffalo are a mountain of bones.
My son is shot for killing their cow.

The Keeper of the Stories – *âcimowinis*

My canoe is swift.
I become a squaw with blood on my hands.

ohkomipan continues the confession

Let them flog.
Enter my parched land.

I am rich. Five dollar every year until I die.
Until the grass die. Until the river die.
Until the sun die. Until
the wind
die.

Squaw marriage. Scrounging.

My son is hung. My father became a skin
slipped through their jail
like a falling star.

Duncan Campbell Scott.
Captured.
Barbed wire.
Squaw in mission school.

Moose milk, my joy.
I am fermented
as the sealers
in their cellar.

The Keeper of the Stories – *âcimowinis*

I will not lose my Pipe.
This holy war I stitch to my dress.
This Skull Dance.
This Ghost Dance.

kahkiyaw iskwêwak, nôtokwêsiwak, câpânak, êkwa
ohkomipanak
Grandmothers, and the Eternal Grandmothers in a
chorus

We are tired, nôsisim – *Grandchild*
The climb down waking our bones.
Your children's tears
roused our sleep.
You have filled our scalped breast
with tobacco.
Our wombs the medicine bags
of your festering.
Listen, nôsisim – *Grandchild*
These stories you gather,
our Sundance songs.
Give me my cane.
I'll awake these sleeping Pipes.
Those Bundles belong to Women,
the wind storms
in the stripes of our flesh.
Our breasts that hang from the belts
of prairie settlers
now sway in the hands of our men.
Oh nôsisim – *Grandchild, we cannot*
carry your burden.
You're youthful,
we are storm-eaten, sun-baked.
We will dance in the teepee
of your children's songs. Dream.
Dream. nôsisim – *Grandchild. Drum.*
Drum. The Medicine lives.
Lives.
Lives.

âcimowinis

Winter rolled from her shoulder,
her song burned.

My fist sunk
in earth. I became a cave
of shredded flesh.

The Keeper of the Sacred Legends – *nôhkom*
âtayôhkan

For centuries
I've tumbled through thistles,
charcoal stars and suns,
groaning lakes and rivers,
my hairy skull
a home for mice and snakes.

A cursed man
chopped up my body,
sent my sons running. Now he swims
in stars,
me dangling in his fist.

I'm earth
born each moon,
waxing and waning,
bleeding eggs.

I'm painted red on rocks;
I swim the caves in lakes
where my head sinks
and I drink to roll again.

The boys have been running.
They are old and wrinkled hearts.
They've eaten leathered flesh.
Knuckles gnawed to the bone,
they run.

The medicines they've thrown
to thorn my path
I've gathered, the Bundles
given to amisk *− beaver,* iskotêw *− fire*
and the swan.
They run from their mother's
nursing tongue.
The flaming open womb,
the burning boiling bone
rolls round and round in
the hairy head.

nâpêsisak, *wailing coyotes,*
run the river bends,
cast your medicines!
nâpêsisak, *wailing boys,*
dust swirls beneath your feet.
The tribal bones
and swimming moon
will fly.

âcimowinis

Elk hide strung on dried wood.
She lifts a bone scraper, the stroke
slides hair to her feet. Thunder rumbles.
Her skin youthful. Voices ragged.

I hold
the wind.

kayâs-âcimowin nôtokwêsiw wîhtam
a grandmother lifted a scraper against a hide, as she
spoke, fur gathered at her feet, the story unfolded

My moccasins carried me across the snow,
my hips horse dancing. My nose against the fog
window, saw him then. His hair the colour
of sun, feet and his legs like moose.
I followed him round and round, watched
the white women, snaking
to look at him.

I waited for him all night in my buffalo robe,
laid against his door.
Still I heard the fiddlers
and laughing dancers.
My wanting saw.
I was driven
by my need of him.
Became frozen.
Gave up everything.

kayâs-âcimowin môniyaw-kisêyiniw wîhtam
an old white man wrung his hands behind his back
his eyes cloud in winter, his faced lined in spring
buds

A bundle of black buffalo
lay at my doorstep. I lifted the corner,
saw her dark eyes, hair sheened
with bear grease
against the piercing snow.

nôtokwêsiw, the Great Granny continues

I lay outside his cabin
night after night, my buffalo robe
wrapped against the wind.
The heat of his breath inside my cloak.
Night after night he came.
Fist raised to his god, lips
pressed against the man hanging dead
around his waist. He entered like a charging
buffalo pounding his chest
against the race of arrows.
I received those spirits.
I lay, my guts exposed,
the loud moan of my need freed
into the night sun. Oh god,
how we sweated in
the thick skin of dead buffalo.
Knives raised and sharpened
clawed and ripped.
Still the buffalo roared,
thundered the sweating pasture.

I don't regret those days, my belly,
swollen with winter feed.
Spring will rise, milk will flow,
a hundred babies rippling
my thighs.
I'd have him again.
I'd have him
again.

môniyaw-kisêyiniw speaks,
The Elderly White man continues,
he is caught in a dream

We had fourteen children. My desire,
I never held it down.
Took in her openness.

âcimowinis

nôhkomak are waking up,
the drum vibrates,
lifts the mass of dawn.
Smoke rises.
The women's blankets spiral
into the Northern Lights.

ohkomipanak. We are Eternal Grandmothers.
We who speak.

I am she who called.
Whispering,
hopeful you might hear.
nôsisimak,
oh don't cry.
We will guide your feather,
dipped in ink.
We will flow.
We will flow.
The well
will never dry.
In those days
we lay heavy
loaded with children, grub.
The men added to our
burden, whipped us
as if we were dogs,
horses ploughing.

We are here.
Here.
Here.
Patience,
nitânisak. *My Daughters.*
We will speak.
We will fill each leaf.
Pages of song.
We will be the loon
in broad daylight
moaning spring.
The deer that rattles her bones.
We will come.
Offer us tobacco,
smudge with sage.
Sit and cry in the Lodge,
let your belly grovel,
let thirst fill your mouth.
We will hold you.
We will fill your lungs.
We will be there.
Sleep.
We will leave our tracks,
laugh through the thunder.
Feel the crack of our whips
will cast lightning,
torch hearts
full of memory.
Listen.

âcimowinis

Her face
mountain river mud.

I pivot.

West.
pahkisimotâhk.
Where the Sun rests.

Forgive me father, I have sinned. I have hauled these
tongues of iskwêwak *since 1492. I no longer know*
which of me speaks.

There were times, nôsisim,
my heart wanted to stop seeing.
I spooned wîhkês *– med-sins into my sister.*
She lay on the ground
filled with homebrew.
Snot covered her baby's moccasin.
That year omikiya *– scabs*
tracked us.

When the snow fall
her spirit go.

I Thirst Dance,
Ghost Dance,
Track Dance,
Chicken Dance.
I Give-Away Dance,
Beaver Dance,
Owl Dance,
Beg Dance.

My moccasins chewed those dances.
My heart gorged. My thoughts slaughter.

kahkiyaw iskwêwak, nôtokwêsiwak, câpânak,
êkwa ohkomipanak.
Grandmothers, and the Eternal Grandmothers wail
in unison

sôhkêyimo. sôhkêyimo.
pimâtisi. âcimostawinân.

Strive in boldness. Strive in strength.
Live.
âcimo.

âcimowinis

Smoke shrouds the dried meat
hanging on a tripod. The sun dips.
She shifts. I puff small winds.
Knee-deep in earth, fingers clawing,
head bobs up and down.
She is there. She is not. A dog howls.

> *I am* câpân, *the grandmother who shamed her family*
> *when sound choked me. Bless me father, this is my sin.*

I watched my people hunched
under their belongings,
worn-out pots, pans clanking.
Babies wailing or asleep in cradle boards.
Bony dogs pulling their travois.
I hear the buffalo hoofs pounding
in their stomachs.

Our men's faces grim,
braids fraying, hair in mud.
Only the young bucks strode,
jaws set for the rising sun.

âcimowinis

And we barricaded them.

It was not the only time
I hated the man
whose white flesh
shared my bed.
My memory snared
by my people, beggars in the land
that once filled their bellies.

I still see those
Grandmothers clench the Bundles,
whisper songs through the night.

> *câpân,* Grandmother, continues strangling, an
> umbilical cord tied her to the earth.

I'd steal flour, sugar, tea,
pass it to my children late at night.
My efforts received by
swollen tongues.
I hung
my husband's twine on
lone tree.

> *âcimowinis*

In the arbour twilight mouth
flags bend, eagles whistle.

The Sky Dancers circle
my head.

kahkiyaw iskwêwak, nôtokwêsiwak, câpânak, êkwa
ohkomipanak.
Grandmothers, and the Eternal Grandmothers
murmur

Squirrels, tall pines, cones, moss.
The jesuits ask do you believe in soul.
When wolves howl, I descend into his mouth.
When coyotes pluck prairie chickens,
I fill his belly. Terra Nullius. Amen.

âcimowinis

My words get in your way.
I feel your sting.
My printer refuses to feed my leaves.
A squirrel stakes out
the sink.
I feed him my apple.
My printer sins.

Father, these robes I wear confuse me. I have forgotten
who I am. A jesuit. A monk. A brother. A priest. A
nun, perhaps. It matters not. I have sinned. My last
confession was in 1492. Yesterday. Ah yes, late today.

I wrote His Eminence,
offered my life to save savage souls.
My mother kissed my crucifix,
said, God go with you.

I am filled with wind, empty forest,
savages peek beneath my robe,
tender hands send heat up my spine.
I bless them.

This whip doesn't bite hard enough, Mother.
I crouch under the cross. Shroud my face.
Swallow. Swallow. Swallow.

This salt water I trickle,
send the Father's Bible thundering.
God be with you.

These savage men – they laugh at my disdain
of their brown-breasted women.
I grind the crucifix. Dry myself.
God be with me.

> *kahkiyaw iskwêwak, nôtokwêsiwak, câpânak, êkwa
> ohkomipanak.*
> Grandmothers, and the Eternal Grandmothers
> proclaim

There are Holy iskwêwak *– nôsisim, all over.*
We were the ones who burned down the jesuits'
church, trilled, danced and laughed through the night.
We watched those cabins eaten by our flames. We
were the ones, nôsisim, *who hid the Bundles,*
held council when we learned how those brothers
lifted their skirts to spill their devils into our sons' night.
And did they think they suffered as they burned,
screaming against our flame?

> *nôhkom âtayôhkan*

I am weary
Snakes dance above my head.
Spit from my womb.
Entwine my legs.
I am not done.

âcimowinis

Sage Woman Eyes with Spirits.
When Thunder speaks,
Lightning flashes from them.
I sit with her in her Lodge.
We cling to our Pipes and weep.
When we weep her tears get up,
become Blue Butterflies.
Mine become Little People
beating their drum.
Butterflies dance.
The Morning Robins lay
their heads to one side
then to the other.
Lift their bustles,
War Dance around our Lodge.
Neither one of us wants to brush away
our tears.

âcimowinis

nimosômak, the four of them
Charlie made a tribe with Sarah,
Willyam made a band with Adeline
Joshwah made a ranch with Bella
mitâtaht, Ten lived with Emma.
They was mens with *asiniyak* – rocks
in their wools, *askiy* – soil in their hands,
the *sîpîsis* – creek in their mouths,
they held our families
together and apart.
Just like –
the womens
they cradled.

> *Bless me father, I have sinned. One of us*
> omosômimâwak *speaks. Though we have remained*
> *silent we too* ê-kiskisiyâhk *– remember.*

When *nimosôm* Bright Eyes waz a boy
he saz da burning of da last *wîhtikow.*
See he hat to die, he said.
When *wîhtikow* roam,
air froze.

Deze days jail fill wit
man who ripped da bums of boys,
eat dere hearts,
bury dem.
All diz dime I dought
dat *wîhtikow* die.

Govern man up is arzs
in Indians.

Dere cowz in bad medzin.
Da buffalo live.
wîhtikow roam.
I build fire,
mak big, big rozes.

kahkiyaw iskwêwak, nâpêwak, kisêyiniwak,
omosômimâwak, âniskotâpânak. êkwa ohkomipanak.
mîna câpânak.
All Women. All Men. All Grandpas. All Great
Grandfathers. Great Grandmothers, the Eternal
Grandmothers. Their Voices form a tight braid

Bless me father, I have killed a few white skins.
I didn't mean to. Forgive me father. I ask for absolution.
I promise to say my rosary and serve my time.
I promise to keep my hands to myself,
swallow my tongue. Amen.

âcimowinis

The spruce we lie on glides.
My fingers
clench dirt. The teepee breathes.
My love's skin slips and slides.
Each thrust
widens the cavern.
We cry like eagles climbing.
I no longer know
who I am.

kayâs-âcimowin nôtokwêsiw wîhtam
A Grandmother sits with a bucket of curdled milk
stirs in strawberries and blueberries while the
thunder calls, she tells

Da factor he always go back to her.
Ever since she come in dat big wood canoe.
Her hair in a big knot her head.
She stand dall like dree.
Her moudth pink like rabbit nose.
I 'member how he put his moudth
on my cheek under dat dree.
I scream an scream. I wand him, now.
I wand him to dake me. An den he put hand
on nipwâm *– kiss me 'gain by da fire.*
I wrap him dere forever.
He go back to her.

I look in big window. He read,
she stand dere dall like dree holding his neck.
I lift his baby to my breast.
He said dey brown jugs. I keep him still. His eyes
dahching my face. My inglish no good.
Me stink of rawhide an burning drum.
Smoke my hair, greased in bear fat.
I no no udder way.
Where I go now I don no. But I go.
Back to bush. Maybe one of my Indian
man dake me an baby. Maybe I dake
no man. Maybe we die.
Snow come soon. I live wit his moudth,
my moudth, my breasts.
I live wit his moudth. Sleep soon.

âcimowinis

Pearls, mango-coloured sand slide from her skin.
Feet calloused from the blood-red stones
of the silver-blue mountains.
How many nights did her Voices
murmur, whisper, cackle rain,
shout, laugh. I lost count.
Days. Nights.
Centuries.

They rub
wedded fingers raw.
Remembered each man's
bruising kiss. The coral wave of
prairie grass, thighs hot.
I am hot. Cold. Goosebumps.
Rain turned to blustering snow
the day I married him.

nôhkom âtayôhkan

Someday I am going back
to be a Lily.

My ribs are brittle,
tired from this strain,
this rock steaming,
pumping, making Suns,
bursting my skin.

I am going back
to be a Lily.

These robes wet, mouldy,
steal space for breathing.

My mouth a wind of souls
dancing the empty night.
I am going back
to be a Lily.
I'll be the thunder stick,
lightning searing my arm.
I'll burst these sheets to dawn.

I am going back.

Along the forest floor
I'll anchor my feet,
step down in the mountain soil.
I'll be swallowed
by muskeg, quickening sand.
Be a Lily.

In these bellies
I'll make my den.
Mouth open,
I'll eat the sun,
dress the moon,
send her
Drumming
your womb.
Oh Yes.

âcimowinis

She petals rain.
Lake waves
swallow. Spit
pebbles. Roll
my tobacco rosary.

She shakes.
Leaves rustle.
Voice husky. Voice
slow. Hard.

My lover's snot
will create my firstborn.
This Pebble.
This Stone.
This Rock.

âcimowinis

okâwîmâwaskiy, *full of grace;*
The Creator is filled with thee;
Blesssed art thou among iskwêwak
and blessed is the fruit of thy womb,
nikâwiy *pray for us* kitânisak,
now and at the hour of our death.
Amen. Amen.

kayâs-âcimowin nôtokwêsiw wîhtam
Wandering Stone Grandmother mouths a corn pipe
pokes holes in heavy smoke circles as she speaks

I've been carrying these little rocks.
My bundle heavy.
I've waited long to move them,
rumbling and roaring,
chipping and polishing
till they've become stones
I cannot lift.

I started collecting
the year I first laid eyes
on the white flesh.
He lay his body on mine.

The seasons are many, each stone
pressed into my flesh.
Sharpen the bone,
pierce my temples, suck till the stones
bleed. They've lain
heavy, so heavy. Too long.

môniyaw-kisêyiniw, an Old Pelt Man rubs
weatherworn hands down his thin wool pants,
and ejects his dreams

I wanted her.
I took her.
My stirring
hovered her mouth.

Wandering Stone Grandmother swallows

This little stone, its heart beats beneath my head.
She sings Chinooks
to break the ice inside my gut.

I place the little stone in a bowl of water,
stirred all night while cinders danced.
At dawn, our bellies full,
we crossed âyimani-sîpiy – *Difficult River,*
energy in our thighs,
laughing at the stumbling redcoats.

môniyaw-kisêyiniw, the Old Pelt Man kicks against
an invisible shore, birchbark canoe wrecked in his
memory

I arrived at the new world sent by the King,
chained and flogged.
I didn't know I'd flee,
the law against my back.
This country where I found my worth.
The savages led me through the valleys.
Promised them whiskey
I'd mix with chewing tobacco, ginger, red pepper,
molasses and a dash of red ink

enough to fill their thirst.

Her, don't believe a word she says.
She's just a toothless squaw
who laid with me after her father died.

Wandering Stone Grandmother weeps her prayer

This stone dropped from my eye.
His fist spoke after my tongue clawed
about the water that caused our men
to spread our thighs, their tongues knives,
vomiting the night.
This stone, its small belly
weighted my infant at Whirlpool Point.
My breasts slaughtered bags
of sweet wine.

môniyaw-kisêyiniw – Old Pelt Man roars

I've no love for girl-childs.
Her mouth's too small, I stifled her yawns,
made my squaw tie her cord.
My squaw. We bucked the night, skins
filled. It's been so long since I've had a woman.
The young boys no longer need to trade.
Her thin legs, tight hold of her buttocks.
I whip, slap till foam drips.
Strange taste of her. I try to be gentle with my
greedy squaw. Fill her
with British blood.

Wandering Stone Grandmother wails.
Voice drifts and bites hard snow.

I was not always cold, tight in heart.
I was not always roped in his fist.
My .22 shot rabbit, grouse, robins,
filled the moment's hunger.

This stone, its white-veined forks
mark the day
my spirit and I
became this stone,
head bowed too heavy to lift.

I was the open flap to all his trades,
my legs unable to walk.
And when he lifted his axe as I slept
my spirit had already gone.

âcimowinis

My bones grate in Sunchild's mouth,
he sucks, spits my seed
and blows me
to the Rocky Mountains.

kimiwan-piyêsîs, Raining Bird,
ran with Spirits in his feet,
redcoats behind him.
He swam the *sôhkêciwani-sîpiy,*
the Fast Flowing River,
heart stronger than the cold
swell of water.

I hold his eyes in my fist,
and when *yôtin-nâpêsis,* Windy Boy,
sweeps the earth,
my fist uncurls.
Sunchild, Raining Bird, Windy Boy,
a finger cut off, the knuckle
grows in weeds
across the Stoneberry Plains.
In Edmonton, *pâspâscês*
searches his scattered blood.

My relatives wake.
Fingers and toes winged,
cord strung in our
infant moccasins.
We've gathered
splintered bones,
weave, mend
the blue marrow.

From Kanesatake, Manitoulin,
Wanuskewin, Maskwachees, Nisgau,
redcoats die beside us.
My Grandfathers' hot breath
bellow songs, scorched eyes
roll their fire in our bellies.

We hunger for those spitted bones.

So many scars.
So many sewed mouths.
Hundreds of Skeletons.
Betty Pamela Rita Gina.

Hold fist in my mouth.
She turns me North.
kîwêtinohk. Where I am
bundled home.

Wandering Stone Grandmother laments

namôya ê-kaskihtâyân
kîkway. kinwêsk.
For so long I have not finished
something.
I've been buried.

Bitterness
eats me. I left too early,
was with him for five winters
before the talk of going over the waters.
One night
I felt the axe.
I watched him
bury me.

A storm, my child, a storm.
I've wandered wailing,
waiting for cistêmâw – *tobacco,*
wêpinâsowin – *flower print*
iyinimina – *blueberries.*
My tongue freed.
The happiness
we shared, his calloused
hands. I too
disappeared like many
of my sisters.
These chained men.
Women, they said, women.
Planted seeds
between our frozen thighs.

kisêyiniw-wâpiskiwiyâs, the old white flesh retaliates

I loved her, this squaw, her little brown body
warmed my bed for a thousand moons. Her
fingers nimble, tanned hides, quick and sharp
in shooting.
I loved her.
When the jesuits came
and cursed her, I never looked at her again.
I drank spirits. Lifted my axe.
I'm bloodstained. And this
British lass is a useless bone.
When I touch her
I remember my little savage,
my brown-skinned whore.
I am stained with her skull.

âcimowinis

My fist festers.
I am cornered.
Haunches ready.

kahkiyaw iskwêwak, nôtokwêsiwak, câpânak, êkwa
ohkomipanak.
All Women. Grandmothers. And the Eternal
Grandmothers testify

They thought they could have as many
as they pleased and we, wanting their flesh,
tasted them. Some took us in our sleep.
Spread us with their hands.
Many bodies tight. We scratched,
lifted our hatches
while our men lay like death,

foul winds grunting,
their spirits trickling.

nôhkom âtayôhkan

I do not exist,
have not
since my bones
dissolved.

âcimowinis

Prayer hits like snow,
wings crashing from the cliff.
I flounder.
My death calls.
I plunge
through the shattered ice-being.
I float
to the crossing-edge.
Fished.
Thawed by prairie hands.

I walked,
my burlap gown blowing.
I met her. She flowed,
weeping birth to a penis.
The teepee sighed
with the twin-tongue spirit.
In sweat I woke, my love
lying limp. I walked back.
The thunderbreeding hills
shattered the lake
where I swam
and swallowed.

I am Gopher Grandmother. Bless me father, I have sinned. Your people have been here for some time and life harbours a long grudge. These are my sins.

My father dreamed
our lifting wails
were the coming winds,
not knowing that when he traded furs
we'd hover in bone –
oskana kâ-asastêki.
He said our winter would be
pelts of thick sky,
no longer weighed down
in buffalo curls.
That year the frog arrived,
my heart wrapped
in thick traders' blankets.
My babies scabbed
in fevered sleep.

Oh little one,
I've become a gopher
jumping hole to hole,
arms too weak to bury
my crusted babies.
My heart a gooseberry
rolling on my tongue.
I have gone with a man
who has a wooden tail,
a grunting guttural grizzly
eats my breast.
I am parched grass
wetting my thirst.
My father's wails long
buried.

âcimowinis

ê-pêcimakik.
I haunt them.
My wailing stories.

Starved Gopher Grandmother wakes the torrential
winds in the depths of her belly as she speaks

My child, your father
is a slop of neck and gizzard.
I brewed ratroot – wîhkês, *rosehips –* okiniyak,
Nettles – masânak, *and sweet bee droppings –* âmow-mêyi,
healed his stink.
Poor man, your father, landing
off the large canoe, fur thick
with lice – ihkwak,
grabbing the earth as if it were a
big-breasted woman, kissing
the cross stick he wore.
I scraped beaver, mink and otter
hides till sun shone off their skin.
I showed him how mosses slept,
winter talked, how pissing
on spruce boughs kept the wolves away.

We spilled with the burden
of those days.
Not once did I hear him
praise the Sun – pîsim, *give thanks*
to Wind – yôtin *and Water Spirit –* nipiy.
Not once did the four-legged people
receive itâskonikêwin.
My blistered skin lies beneath
large beads and wooden sticks,

his whispers whipping.
My child, your father's
closing eyes and leaving wind
is my mending. He crossed
the other side long before
I became his wife.

âcimowinis

In this frozen woods,
the warmth of the wood stove,
the calling-going-away snow falls.
I am cocooned one hour from the city,
writing.
I watched the two winds fighting
who would rule the spring.
They ripped branches,
cascaded snow,
charged and rolled
in the grooves of footprints
snowmobiles tracked from the frozen lakes.
I hung onto my sheets,
cowed in my electric blanket.
When the Voices roar,
I write.
Sometimes they sing,
are silent.
In those times
I read, answer overdue letters,
go for a walk or jog,
stoke my fire, prepare baloney
mustard sandwich, wild rice salad.

ê-pêcimakik.
I haunt them.
My wailing stories.

pê-nîhtaciwêk, nôhkomak.
Climb down, my Grandmothers.

Before the thought is done
they know my prayers.

> *kahkiyaw iskwêwak, nôtokwêsiwak,*
> *câpânak, êkwa ohkomipanak.*
> All Women. Grandmothers and Eternal
> Grandmothers, they scold with a wind
> that shakes leaves.

We do not talk until we are fed.
You've wanted us yet you ignore us.
Dream us.   Feed us.
Child Woman.

> *âcimowinis*

Saskatoon moose nose sturgeon soup
Indian popcorn bannock lard
laced bowels bible tripe duck
neck bones deer steak goose roast
cottage cheese cream tea
corn rice raisin strawberry pudding.

> *Bless me father. I am Grandmother Bargain. These*
> *are my sins. Forgive me father for I have wanted...*

Fur covered ohkwâkan
his eye big heaven – oskîsik,
sky and river waves.
Raining mouth, his breath
a foreigner.

54

Hands – micihciya,
feathers sweeping.
I couldn't tear away.

I stayed at our teepee
pitched far from the fort.
Boiled reed – wahotêw
mînisa – *berries,*
dried meat – kâhkêwak
and askipwâwa.
You, nicawâsimis,
tucked in shawls,
sucking your thumb,
wide-eyed.
Like your father
you kept watch.

I couldn't stand
the sweet white-skin women.
Afraid those
fur-lined faces
would devour my spirit.
I oiled with cottonwood.
Waited in buckskin
for the forest lakes,
evening heat.
You, nicawâsimis,
in your cradle board.

My father saw
my future husband –
mounds of fur,
flour – aski-pahkwêsikan
tea – maskihkîwâpoy *and*
sugar – sîwinikan,
kettle – sîsîpaskihk
knives – môhkomâna

and guns – pâskisikana.
He saw
deer-skinned children
laughing,
his knees wobbled in wind.

I, his youngest,
with a squirrel's tongue,
beaver-paw hands,
elk's hips, deer walk,
burned deep from the sun,
fresh berry blood.
I became the trade.

My father said the man's eyes
travelled the teepee flaps,
danced with stars.
He said the man's hands
were rawhide,
robins preening.
His mouth tugged when he said
my feet would travel
rivers and my heart
bleed our song.

nicawâsimis,
though the day
sat on my shoulder,
my yôtin *was purple,*
big heavens swam the rapids.
I looked beyond the grass,
became the beaded belts
of my father's dream.

âcimowinis

Young and old women sit in a semicircle.
Hands on each steamed bowl, pot and pan.
My face mascara-smeared. To each I say,
You have come. Pray. *kâkîsimo. ayamihâ.*

> *kahkiyaw iskwêwak, nôtokwêsiwak, câpânak, êkwa
> ohkomipanak.*
> Grandmothers and the Eternal Grandmothers
> affirm

*We glued and laced
wombs, ribs built.*

âcimowinis

Diamond-squared blankets
washboards basins utensils
tea kettles needles beads.
I scatter gifts. The hungry
rush. Food. Gifts. Hand to hand.
The Drumming begins.

> Count My Blessings Grandmother, another
> blasphemy

*I wasn't dead when he took his white bride.
Didn't I tell you all along I've been a breeding
horse galloping. Fed to dogs,
I rotted.*

How many times as I lay beneath him
did he remind me
I am the bargain from my father's trade?
How many times did he raise my dress,
sweated hands smeared with dirt and cow,
bloody from skinning? And I
received him joyfully.

I am
a gentleman's wife.

At the trading post the factors and
their knowing slide down my belly,
lay their needles, run
their hands on satin.
Yes, the forest and its creatures
house my flesh.
I have not learned to chime
like their bells
nor move like our canoes.

I've scrubbed with ashes,
still my skin is baked. Oh yes, it's true
he treated me and our children kindly.
He wings in forest, his heart stays in britain
and when his cousin frances
comes along,
he's gone.

I've lived in this shack,
raised our children,
fed by my neighbour's husband,
the small portions
he left for us at the bay.
I hold my beads.
Before I sleep.

I lay traps.
Hide behind trees.
Hands on my mouth.

âcimowinis

The Drumming. Chorus. Wolves.
Stalk my den. Food eaten. We dance
and dance and dance.

> *kahkiyaw iskwêwak, nôtokwêsiwak, câpânak, êkwa*
> *ohkomipanak*
> All Women, Grandmothers and Eternal
> Grandmothers, *kâkîsimo,* in a ceremonial chant
> they encourage

êy êy êy nôsisim
here this needle
thread its eye
oh these *âcimowinisa* –
stories so small
pull them out
squeeze them through

êy êy êy nôsisim
some songs
come tumbling out
weak and small
êy êy êy nôsisim

âcimowinis

They sing me to *kîwêtinohk.*
North. They bundle me home.
A rag wick flicks.
I'll never smell *wâpikwaniya* again,
hear *piyêsîs* sing,
feel *pîsim*'s heat.
My feet blister to their path.

âcimowinis

My Grandmothers were country wives –
bartered, traded, stolen, bought and sold
sometimes loved by
Frenchmen – *mistikôsiwak*
Englishmen – *âkayâsiwak*
Ukrainians – *opîtatowêwak*
Norwegians
Irishmen
Scotsmen

I do not recognize who speaks.

I give you these offerings
from their *âcimowina* and tie tobacco
to their ribs.

Born in a Dent Grandmudder stutters her story

Our feet were free
before da walk of da white skin.
I can't dell you where I waz born.
In a dent somewhere,
maybe in da bush. Mudder
squat an push.
The wind – yôtin
scream and scream.
But not Mudder.

My mudder and fudder were liddle bid Irish
an French. My grandfudder, dough, he dick
dough white skin speak grandmudder's Cree.
She, grandmudder, was a pure. I 'member dere
stories. You grandfudder he dell you first.

Old Grandfather Trader he want her he speaks

I was a French lad
used to ramble boat to boat.
Little chore here, little chore dere,
earn me livin', wine, women.
I'd live on pork. I work ard,
got my hands to show it.

Everytime we turn a corner 'round dem lakes da land stop
my breating. Over each ill we climb, god's and stretch more
dan our eye can see. Old Women's Lake. Where the Moose Died.
Dried Meat ills. I pull my rosary an dank da god for dem sky
an ills. Swear da devil when we suffer from wads of mosquito,
sandflies, noseeums, horseflies. Somedime go hungry for days.
Plenty animals but our hunters waz clomping trough dem woods
scare da by jezuz outta da mooze. Da savages waz good to us.
Drezz in dem furs an skins an hide, faces paint. Not one fat savage,
dough can't say any one of us waz ever in lard. I see many
change in my dime.

Dem jezuits had it in dem to make da savage holee, didn't like
dere wild chantin', smokin' dem grazz an makin' dere mozez
speakin' to dem bushes an round rocks. I'm little blind now
but I still see kôhkom, *in dat water hole. Didn't no I was*
watchin'. Maybe snare me like rabbit if she no. We'd sneak.
Dey had eyes like hawk, ears like wolf, but we use deze long
stalk wit large eye. I see trough them willow. Yes. My man
want her. I not a rich fellow in dem days but I work hard
had me some chevaux, i dired of sewin' me own hide,
dired of me cold bedroll, my cabin could use fresh bannock
an smell of woman. Never mind she greaze wit animal lard,
make it eaze for trappin'. An doze elk teeth she wear on
her breast, well dat's all right too.

Born in Tent Grandmother *kiskisiw* –
her memory stirs

Yes, kimosôm, *his doughts dake many paths,*
memory full. Liddle string died to dat liddle string.
I dravel wit him, crossed dat sôhkêciwani-sîpiy.
Dere we watch butterfly swallows. Swarms an swarms
makin' a blanket of tiger lily. He said dem old savages
use to dell him fellow like im a lonesome warrior.
Dey cry for der nîcimos, *an der* nîcimos *woman*
would dance trough dat butterfly flower. Dere earts
would sing, dey no dere woman is safe an soon dere
finger meet. I dought dat somedime soon I see
nîcimos *sing love song in dem trees across da river.*
When we stand by dat swollen stealin river an da
butterfly dance, we no to paddle soft an swift.

âcimowinis

Sing. Sing, *nôhkomak.*
Lend me your wind.

Over the prairie
her Voice rolled.

kahkiyaw iskwêwak, nôtokwêsiwak,
câpânak, êkwa ohkomipanak.
All Women. Grandmothers and
the Eternal Grandmothers beseech

êy êy êy nôsisim
here this needle
thread its eye
oh these âcimowinisa –

stories so small
pull them out
squeeze them through
êy êy êy nôsisim
some nikamowinis
come tumbling out
weak and small
êy êy êy nôsisim
kika-pîcicînânaw
your fingers
stitch this cloth
mend these moccasins
light my ospwâkan
êy êy êy nôsisim
so long we've sat
êy êy êy nôsisim
we've waited for so long.

âcimowinis

I've folded this five dollar
till I've made the Queen's
ass smile.
I take her North
where her promises
wait.

Not So Long Ago Granny Wants to Get Even rages

I'll have a bunch of dem,
hus' been, wives.
As many as my fingers.
Kill lotsa deer,
have lotsa baby.
Dat'll put dem back
on dem big canoe.

Dem go home.
My big family
make dem go home.
Yes.

âcimowinis

A chameleon. Round dancing,
the Give-Away. I lift my feet.
For Usne Josiah. Omeasoo Kirsten Marie.
Josiah Kesic. Alistair William Aski.

Wild rice pine nuts
coke potato chips baloney steak
lobster dried meat rabbit kidney tripe
earl grey cappuccino mint muskeg tea.

Moccasins sneakers high heels hiking boots
jeans buckskin miniskirts ribbon dress gowns.

Stoneboats wagons horses cadillac
hondas volkswagen sedan cruise ship
mustang jeep ford tractor four-wheel drive jet planes.

Roy Orbison Hank Williams k.d.lang Otis Redding
Mosquito Drums Buffy Sainte-Marie Kashtin Murray Porter
Zamfir Enya B.B. King Glen Gould Riccardo Muti.
Maytag wood stove outhouse bathroom bush
high-rise apartment house tent teepee sweat lodge.

wîsahkêcâhk wîhtikow Long Stocking
Shakespeare Jung Pablo Neruda
Louise Erdrich Mary Daly Maria Campbell.

kahkiyaw iskwêwak, nôtokwêsiwak,
câpânak, êkwa ohkomipanak.
All Women. Grandmothers and the Eternal
Grandmothers in a surge they reproach

ê-ma-môniyâskwêhkâsoyâhk.
We act like white women,
our brothers, sons said.
môniyâs *made white squaws out of us.*
They laugh at our tea gatherings.
Said our môniyâs *rich and stingy,*
we no longer needed their offerings.

Though we loved those men we slept with,
those our fathers traded us to
for buckets of moose milk, scrip,
we wept into ashes we scrubbed
into their wood floors.
Our white husbands lay beside those
white women they yearned for.
We hoarded the medicines,
beaded our stories into quilts,
stitched into sinew. Our children
would never know the bitter
cold of white hands,
never know the slapping sting
of our brothers' words.

When that five dollar came,
one for each Indian,
we the Squaw brides
stood along the sidelines,
no longer the Mothers
of this land.

Petticoat Grandmother, her voice ice-droplets
and spring rain

My teeth have dropped
from years of tanning hide, but
I lift that teacup, proper-like,
and my breast are bound.
I know the fiddle dance.
My petticoat
a wind behind my steps.

In the outskirts of this village,
I watch my brothers, sons
whip the horses, covered wagons.
Madam
sits by the man who shares my bed,
her bonnet flying.
Flaming cheeks, rabbit-stained
lips by his side.
I will not have a thing like that
inside my body,
she said when I asked her
when my relative was to be born.
And though I am no longer
the bride,
my moccasins
fly.

Keeper of the Stories – *âcimowinis*

They hobbled, limped, shuffled,
pink, purple, blues, reds, yellows,
white, black, printed blazed
calico dresses, shawls,
kerchiefs, blankets.

Dried flowers, old sweat
and sweet perfume, they teased,
laughed, joked and gossiped.
Ran their fingers through each
swinging hand. Pipe smoke
swirled. Men drumming our songs.

I watch them. Hundreds of my husband's family.
They've travelled across Canada, the United States,
rejoice at recognizing one another, some for the first time.
Each has brought a book they've lovingly compiled.
It contains the history of their migration
from England, Norway, and into the Dakotas.
They are scattered throughout Turtle Island.
They marvel at the trek of their ancestors.
The click of wine glasses echoes through the arbour
of this large family gathering. And five Indians.
I the eldest, my children and two other Indian youth.
They are not yet aware how this affects their lives.
Who are we? Adopted. I gather inward.
How many of my relatives were cattled
onto the reservation during their settlement?
How much of my people's blood was spilled
for this migration? Laughter and wonder
as fingers move across the atlas. This is where
great-granddad Arne crossed on the barge.
This is where great-great-granddad travelled
and preached the law of the land where his
wife Isobel taught the little savages to read.
My lips are tight from stretching when my
small family is introduced alongside the
large extended family. Later,
driving home, I weave a story for my children –
how their great-grandma rode sidesaddle,
waving her .22 in the air trying to scare

those relatives away. I tell them
how my relatives lived around the fort,
starving and freezing,
waiting for diluted spirits
and handouts from my husband's family.
I tell them
how their little children died wrapped in
smallpox blankets.
My breath
won't come anymore.
I stare
at the wheatfields.

kahkiyaw iskwêwak. kahkiyaw nâpêwak.
nôtokwêsiwak. câpânak. êkwa ohkomipanak.
omosômipanak.
All Women. All Men. Grandmothers and
Eternal Grandmothers. Eternal Grandfathers.
Their memory filled their bucket as if fingers
were shifting through blueberry leaves. They
stained their hands. Cranberries burst on tongues.
Chokecherries thickened throats. Saskatoons wept
as they slipped into moose nose soup. Raspberries
and strawberries burned against steamed rocks.
These Voices remembered.

Grandfather bent over the paper leaves,
knife with pâskisikana – guns stand by.
This day and many others
I've wanted those guns
pointed, hard and straight.

We were eating summer pups,
buffalo heaped in sour heat –
no rabbits,

no berries
to fill our dying bellies.
Our warriors crying,
the Sundance Tree
fall
from the pâskisikana.
Ghost Dancers in
bleeding shirts.
We were dying. We were
dying. Dying.

Grandfather talked
with Grandmother. She said,
"River blood will always be our milk.
This talk will stain the leaves."

Grandfather carried his bending,
joined the other walk-far eyes.
They shared the Pipe.
This is how it came to be.
Grandfather drawing suns
moons
lakes
winds and grass.

âcimowinis

Snot rainbow babies
Parliament chieftains.
Fancy dancers. Symphony.
Drummers. Ballerina.

I will breed.
Everywhere.

kahkiyaw iskwêwak. nôtokwêsiwak. câpânak,
êkwa ohkomipanak.
All Women. Grandmothers
and Eternal Grandmothers endure

mâto, nitânis
Cry, my daughter.
The leaves have not collected our dust,
the veins crumpled into soil.

We do not exit
except in the open mouth
of sky. No voices
dream our Visions.
We fly in the blood – *kiwîcisânihtonâwâw*
of you *nitânisak.*
My daughters.

âcimowinis

My Grandfather laughs,
takes my fingers
through the thick black book.

He swam *mistasinîwi-sîpiy* – the Big Stone River.
His moccasins ran
red, white, grey, the blacks rocks,
a bowl of sweet smoke, spiral
willow, singing his songs.

In Rocky Boy Reserve my relatives drum
songs of Raining Bird, Windy Boy,
Sunchild. White-braided brides
deliver Bundles.
Bones wrapped in red
cloth, tobacco, twisted hair,

miles and miles
across the prairie. The Belly River.

My Grandmother's hips
roll past the drums,
fingers playing, hair kissing lips,
ash rises, their sweeping feet.

The remains of chapels burning,
chalices gleaming,
scalps, smallpox, famine
and winter sleeping.
My Grandmother's shrill
fingers in the thick leather book.

This walking dance,
this running dance,
gathers pencil scratch
over the lines,
empty bellies fill with all
my Saints.

ê-pêcimakik.
With my sorrow,
I call you.
Haunt us
with your cries.

âcimowinis

Grandmother was a breed
who loved to raise her
petticoat to the Red River Jig.
That's what Auntie Mud said.

nôhkom Michif does not apologize

Snowshoes and walking stick, we cross
winter-starved lakes,
jaws crack, groan.

Whisky-jacks hop our shoulders,
chattering for intestinal fat
hanging from our rolled packs.

Our little girl is a snowshoe hare.
She crunches crusty snow, mates
with the gust.
Beaver, muskrat, mink traps
clank in rhythm of our toboggan.

We cross today.
Soon spring will dig rivers, lakes,
carts, sucked in mud.
Tonight we'll be at the settlement.

Tomorrow when the sun dives
we'll river jig,
eat steamed pudding,
cream and curdled milk.

I'll scrub in Lopotash, curl in
my husband's arms,
sing loud my Michif.
Wake the whole Metis.

Tonight we are Free
from eyes that look at us –
fencing.
Rifles cradled.

âcimowinis

My Grandmother would fly
with the humming roll
of her tongue.
ê-mamâhtâwisit.
She is gifted
with arrival.

The day the government agents
starved the people at Frog Lake
men paid with their breath. News
travelled fast.

Beads dangling,
she hummed, her feet
hummingbird's wings.
Two days of running
from our reserve.

Agents escaped dressed like women.
She guided them through thundering trees.
When that bloody battle was over
Grandmother lay. Tongue ripped.
Today at Frog Lake she sits. Barred

at the trading post. She watches.
Bits of paper signed, hundreds
of names,
provisions and hocking of wares.
Hungry belly. Sleeping spirits.

And them priests pitch
wailing tents, talking tongues,
bibles,
writhing warriors.

> *sîpi-kiskisiw Grandmother* – Long Term Memory
> Grandmother speaks as if she's sucking on a
> cracked thigh bone, she draws out the marrow

Mother buried wîhtikow.
Never let me forget those
starving nights,
how her ribs lived.
She weighed no more than a
coyote
feeding on mice.

Father was a good man,
kept me on my feet.
His people slaughtered
my mother's family.

My Grandfather watched
the flutter of the paper leaves
as spirit feather woke its
treaty promise. He
fought with lance and arrow,
rotted behind bars
his treaty coat
a shredded ribbon.

âcimowinis

I laid my palm on the heated
Agawa Rocks. The serpent rose,
its bloody guts crashed against
my hand.

> *kahkiyaw iskwêwak, nôtokwêsiwak,*
> *câpânak, êkwa ohkomipanak.*
> All Women. Grandmothers and Eternal
> Grandmothers. From the depths of waters
> where legends sleep and grow, these Voices wake

We are a ball of skulls, skins
gnawing against our bones.

> *kahkiyaw nâpêwak, kisêyiniwak, câpânak,*
> *êkwa omosômipanak.*
> All Men. Grandfathers and Eternal Sleep Grand-
> fathers. From the depths of currents and streams
> where fingerlings swim, these Voices tremor

My wife claws open her forearm,
her warmth drips
into my mouth.

> *nôhkom âtayôhkan*

I am the serpent
coiled
in beaver dams.
The hunched sturgeons moving
cave to cave,
lake to lake.

kahkiyaw nâpêwak, kisêyiniwak, câpânak,
êkwa omosômipanak.
All Men. Grandfathers and Eternal Sleep
Grandfathers, their water-voices are fire

I sit in the Lodge, listen
to my wife's bursting,
wet her with my tongue,
crack my bone,
feed her marrow.

nôhkom âtayôhkan

I am the stalker of bear, buffalo,
the coil in jesuits' dream.
I am the Lodge
within my bone,
coil in the jesuits' dream.
I am the flogging whip.
Coil, jesuits, dream.
I am the blood.
Coil, jesuits.
Coil.

âcimowinis

The wind has mouth.
Water arms. Rocks feet.
Sun face. The pale skin
wanders. Sleepless.
While the Sweat Lodge
bursts.

Rainbow Grandmother re-visions

The last time my lover held me,
tongue in my ear,
my Indian bride, my dirty breed
walk to my brother's lodge.
When his relatives came
I hid my moccasins.
His brother asks for the love
medicine. Herbs and roots.
Should I guess what his woman
said when she left?
"It was the way your pleasure lit up
when you spoke in that cultured way.
It was the way your hand lingered
over her soft white ones.
I cannot tell you how I am lost.
My hands, words, caught
in the door of your schools.
My winter lard waltzes to my shame."

The first time I met him,
he claimed me.
I am a breed
who believes
the Rainbow sings.

âcimowinis

Thunderbirds woke me.
Wings flapping against their dance,
slamming doors, crashing windows.
I tucked my head.
Sliced fingers on these musty papers
where I singed their feathers.

Their lore washes my skin, my blood
fresh food. I am scalded.
Coiled anger licking.
I'll move along the grass, hot, wet,
flex my muscles, receive the swallow's
tongue. The fingers that hold
my heart, fluttering butterflies, pull
me to the Thunder Ice Bird Beings.
I am frail, withered speech,
stick to their touch. I haul one foot,
a buffalo hoof, the other
tickled by their dance. I travel
a crippled being, hold my Pipe,
cry for my return.
I travel their lustful cries clawing,
tearing my burn.

I'll travel this fierce storm,
slam my own doors,
palms open to the throb
of my own heart.

My father's dubious eye looks.
I crawl into him,
drag out his tongue.

I cannot name him.
Will not name him. My poor father.
He is many fathers.

Nameless *pâpâ* calls upon his daughter to join him
in his memory

Do you remember the small clearing there
on the hill
surrounded by pine trees?
The slough where we collected water.
Where the singing snakes swam.
Do you remember the tent we pitched?
You slept with your pig while everyone
worked? The square hole
of straw and dirt
you kids squeezed between your toes
for plastering the cabin? Even the smallest child
had a hand sawing, stripping bark off the logs,
plastering mud, placing sod.

âcimowinis

I used to walk up the hill
to look at the hole
where the cabin
lived.

I cannot name him.
Will not name him.
My poor father.
He is many fathers.

Nameless *pâpâ* continues the autumn remembering

The first christmas while you were all gone
I nailed slats, buried
your small footprints.
I waited
for your return.

Do you remember how the bird sat
outside the windowsill, chirping?
You were her "land of little sticks."
She flew into your mouth before she died.
Indian Affairs
took you before your wings unfolded.

I remember hauling my mattress
from the dormitory the day they served fish.
We'd empty the crushed straw in the pigpen.
In the barn we'd load our mattress with fresh hay.
Bodies bundled, we chiselled ice
in the creek that ran a mile from boarding school.
Always frozen, those days. And now, my girl,
you complain about wood hauled through the seasons,
how I stoke your tent stove.
My bones in winter.

They took you.
I met them at the door.
Your mother told you how wîsahkêcâhk tossed his eyes.
He broke the little bird's rule
and his eyes wouldn't come back.
She spun this story, rubbed your belly
till you slept.

I stood beneath those pine trees,
our cabin won't be cold.
Sawing, chopping, my shirt soaked.
My ears didn't hear chirps that day.

When I curled against your mother, cradled her,
her eyes stung.
We never spoke of that raking storm.
The spirits in my fists. My stomach brewing.

Each raging blow –
Indian Affairs, priest and nuns –
blizzards in my autumn pain.
Your mother's laughter, dancing
in chicken coop, pigpen.

In the sugar-beet fields you'd hoe,
five rows you'd slash. I'd meet you from the other end,
determination on your sunflower face. I saw the span
of your fledgling wings, songs colouring all your dreams.

And though I strained my eyes, my ears, opened my arms,
you walked ahead. I on homebrew, digging sandwiches
on 97th street, smoking lipstick-stained butts.

Now you tell me
as you hold my cigarette-tarred hands
I've been killing myself since you were a child.
These hands, I cannot lift them to your face.
I am snowbound in my stone smoked walls,
my belly leaks into this waltzing woman.
your mother an Elder's bride.
And you ask me,
Papa, what was it like for you?

âcimowinis

Your birthday comes, father. I have nothing
to offer. You sit in your smoke-filled
room, hold a cigarette at the tip of
your stained finger. Bring it to
your cautious lips.

You tell me you were born when
the chokecherries grew plump and tart,

after the first pain of frost.
nôhkom squeezed milkstone, mixed Indian Popcorn,
boiled turnip and rabbit as if *nimosôm* never came
home empty-handed. That milkstone was from the spring,
and grey as clouds that promised rain.
You always thought *nôhkom*'s magic saved you,
my uncles and aunts, from ripping roaring guts.
Just the way she would grind and brew herbs
for healing.

I work to bury your fist, my father, my tongue
a willow whipping your clenched hands. I cry
for a hundred blessings to wash your grimacing
face. Our relatives cross the river through
sifting sand. There they lifted you.

Staring out the smudged, smoke-filled window,
you hold your waltzing woman, pants smelling
like stray dog. Nothing reflects back. Just
a sad jalopy filled with people smoking, cackling
over spilled wine. Not long ago you sat with them,
pockets singing coins collected table to table
at the Cecil hotel. You lift your fist, swear at
your god, while your babies
milk books.

Slosh that beer, that cheap wine
on the tabernacle, the fathers,
sister superior, the pope,
lay your trap in front of Indian Affairs,
vomit what is left of your empty gut,
stench them, they who
saturated blood,
whipped your spirit,
oh my broken father.

kahkiyaw iskwêwak, nôtokwêsiwak,
câpânak, êkwa ohkomipanak.
All Women. Grandmothers and Eternal
Grandmothers, tender hands, soft breathing,
moisture fills these words

I hear him, nôsisim
these fossiled bones
cradle his fevered heaves.
êy êy êy nôsisim
these medicines thaw
our murdered wounds
êy êy êy nôsisim.

âcimowinis

Indian Affairs. Gave me a one-way
ticket. When Grandmother died
I stayed picking butts, scrounging
nickles and dimes. In valleys
lechers, whores and pimps
bought cheap wine,
filled rubbers,
I sloshed my sins.

When the alarm clock rang
I emptied bedpans, fresh ice water,
lined up tumblers for withered hands.
Hallways, piss, liniment,
a trolley full of guts.
When I left, my Grandmother
had filled my pockets full of
peppermint. I ate all of them.
Filled my fist with my father's
walk.

Walking sterile hallways,
computers flickering, I held
my pencils, books.
My father squeezed
in my fingers.
A bag full of Sally Ann
bikini briefs, bras.
I stuck my thumb
to the mountains,
tents and horses
where my parents lived.

For miles my father and I
walked. Cans, beer bottles,
filled a jalopy full of pennies.
Drank spirits. Mother and I
held our breath a hundred miles
across the *sôhkêciwani-sîpiy* –
the Fast Flowing River.
A brewing storm of metal boots
broke mother's bones,
set my stomach heaving.

She sheds buckskin. Hightops.
Loosen braids. The Ages
become my mother. Arms
raised. She sings.

I will not name her.
Cannot name her.
She becomes everyone's
mother.

Nameless *mâmâ* sings in a clear and mournful chant

waniskâ
pê-wâpan ôma
âsay piyêsîsak
nikamowak
miyohtâkwan
kitaskînaw.

âcimowinis and *mâmâ* sing

waniskâ
Arise

pê-wâpan ôma
dawn has come

âsay piyêsîsak
already the birds

nikamowak
sing

miyohtâkwan.
the beautiful song

kitaskînaw.
our land.

âcimowinis

nôhkom's skunk drapes my chair.
I lean against it, the ancient smell,
bottles that lined her window. Spill

into air with which I wrestle. On my father's
bed absorbine junior, ice cool liniment.
Players light, export a, number 7,
bingo dabber. Sweet grass and sage.

Ukrainian music sweeps his room.
The wall is covered with my family's smiles.
My brother and sister, their families missing.
Not long ago the three of us sat
at his hospital bed. My brother reading
the edmonton journal, my sister asleep.
Me prattling. His eyes a tiny light.
He tells me the sons of bitches thought
they had won when they gave him a box
of shells, whiskey, a treaty number and
a bit of land. His guts exposed, he laughs,
fighting with a cousin about that land.

Last I saw him, he sat unshaved,
belly button black, elbows plastered.
I had nothing to say.

âcimowinis

I cannot name her.
Will not name her.
She becomes everybody's
mother.

Nameless *mâmâ* chews *wîhkês* – a bitter root –
as she speaks

I want to kick doze jesus out, boot you fudder in da ass,
his face fallin' to da floor an creep da night.
I want to dake da rifle an shoot
doze jesus out, you fudder, we went to boarding scold
but him he laid down his moudth
an only poured da spirits in.
When he dought dat udder man
douch my spoon his boot an fist come fly,
even dought da jesus spend his dime dere.

kikiskisin cî? *Do you 'member*
da âcimowina *about* wîsahkêcâhk? *I dold you dat story*
dat night. Even dough you didn't no what doze jesus
said, you eyes no dat look of ugly spirit in you fudder's eye.
You ears no dat story of woman hide in bush. No place to hide.
I rub you belly sleep, burn large wood, our cabin durned cold.
In bed I rub my fingers into da dirt, wet da mud deep
in my pillow. I die dat night.

An den you leave.
I burn deep holes. I fill dem like you fudder.
Sleep wit dem jesus. I hide in kerchief, eyes mud-stain
an dis dam I wear since doze days I spend in scold.
Dat rifle, my dream. I fist dem jesus
dill dey scream, legs dwisted, broken like deze scars.

Arms empty like mine when you leave.
An when you come, you still gone.
Da words you speak, da man you marry, da dress you wear,
not da bush I dought I plant in you feet. An you ask about
doze days. I dell you I milk dem cows good, squirt milk pail
like no buziness, mak strong head cheeze, da ukraniums
daught me bore-sh, an bake sin a man roll, jelly roll. Hokay.
Have I dold how my heart roll in my belly,
how I eat an eat to keep it still,
an you call me fat porcupine, fat round beaver.
My head always feel you fudder's fist,
no aspirin,
no doctor.
No medsin man
can dake dat away. An you want me
to dell about long ago story. Dem big fights, you
grandfudder's smart, run wit da women to Rocky Boy.
Dat's why we go visit
Small's, Windy Boy, Raining Bird, Sunchild, Fanny,
Liz-bet. Hokay?

          âcimowinis

Mother leans against the door frame.
She seeks the sun. She folds her hands behind
her back, head covered with a red tam.
The distant weeping wakes agony in her arms.
Burning rice, raisins. She hibernates. Wind
gripes her. She no longer knows if her
asthma is acting up as she wipes her face.

She remembers another doorway, waving.
Cheap stupor burping, she watches
her daughter drive away. Grandchildren's
faces pinched against the car window.

In the early years,
the crooked good sired
trails of wounds,
still the mother's bead.
The rains blessed them.
Everywhere visitors gather
a crying relative lodge waits.
Its bent willows
weighed down by traders'
blankets. Inside steam rocks
raise humble wails,
our prayer.

Nameless *mâmâ*, as the years pass, her English improved though as she re-entered childhood the Old Cree hibernated in her nest again. For now she is in her mid-life

They stay away. My life filled with husbands who pawed
my children, slammed fist into their hides, my arms pining,
my tongue mute. I bead moccasins, gather moss for the
cradle board. Still the loon dives into my Lodge. The
woodpecker knocks. Next time I see nôsisimak,
we talk like squirrel and fox.

My window is a smear of greasy neck bones. Finger
my heart. Tomorrow I offer print, tobacco when the
sun comes. Pray. Sing Morning Song. Pray my
daughter comes.

âcimowinis

Four winters we live in a red brick house.
Milk delivered, sometimes receive a package
of pemmican or dried meat. My children and I
inhale. I'd weave stories. Mother jigging.
Mother speaking Michif, cleaning berries.
Mother mixing flour paste for cardboard
walls. I'd search for Cree on the radio,
walk the valley with my little ones,
picking chokecherries. I'd crush till
I burst all over my canvas. The train
moves too slowly. Baby against my breast.
I hold my little boy's hand.

I will not name her.
Cannot name her.
She becomes everyone's
mother.

Nameless *mâmâ* observes the distance between the
bush snares, and walking. Residential school and
freedom. Sadness fills her.

The house echoes. nôsisim*'s out of his moss bag*
running in puddles. His lakes filled with ships, jet planes.
Green eyes and straw blond hair shrink from my dark skin.

âcimowinis

At the women's cultural centre
Mother and I build our Lodge,
hold ourselves.

I will not name her.
Cannot name her.
She becomes everyone's
mother.

> Nameless *mâmâ* is filled with lakes that crush her
> chest and overwhelm her big skies.

Kesic, my great-grandson, is like his grandpa. His eyes bluer.
At the Round-dance he wants no other than his grandmother.
My daughter carries him round to each relative. Lifts him high.
I've long worn out my moccasins. I'll carry these memories
deep in my Bundle.

âcimowinis

She wears her apron eating pork,
neck bones, bannock and lard. She uses
a prying knife, carves every crevice. Sucks
marrow making pucker sounds. She
mixes a pot of day-old porridge, swishes
the bone mix for her dogs. My mother.

Sweet grass lingers on her bedroom walls.
The basement, the smell of many loved, dead
cats. Outside the reserve, dogs, their
constant erections, lick their jowls. Always
hungry, their ribs cling. Bones scatter the yard.
A slab of bacon hangs on the clothesline for the
chickadees. Garbage heaped on a platform.

She digs in her fridge where white lard is mixed
with stains of raspberry jam, exposed stew turns
black, a jar of cream withered and mossed.
She expects me soon so she keeps it.

She yearns to eat. Rabbit, deer, moose
nose, porcupine, beaver, muskrat, prairie
chicken. She wants fat. Must have fat.
Dried fat from the insides of cows.
Large gut fat from moose. She will hang
it above her skin after scrubbing the blood
and gristle off. The flies will gather,
feast, and she'll hang a sticky flycatcher.
Trapping. She'll hoard all of it. Walk
the night. Stalk her fridge again and again.

In my freezer I keep fresh neck bones, kidneys.
I buy her thick slices of Italian bread. She
hates it. She hands me her head,
thick sour memories.

In my office her fingers snap,
withdrawing from spotted painted snakes,
green and silver, Aborigine snakes.
I've done this on purpose. She knows.
We laugh.

nitânisak

We are collectors.
The most frail carries a pail
she hangs from her belly,
filled with roots, bark, rock
insect legs, butterfly wings.
She wears them.
Butterfly wings, stuck with safety pins,
hundreds on a rag blanket.
Roots around her skate blades,
wings flap along the creek.
She plasters cedar, goose grease,

birch bark against her breast.
Yes, wears them,
insects filing their legs on her tailbone,
siblings crying for her Bundles,
fingers too thin to hold the scrapes
of sunlight she moulded with her spit.

In a buffalo-mildewed lodge
lies a woman plucking,
dancing moons swimming marrow.
Spider babies fill her mouth,
spin on tender willow,
drag her skeleton
torched with red lightning,
green thunder, rain star light.
She sings, and sings.
Bones flush the night.

The old one binds ribs, moose gut,
gristle basket spun from her waist.
In the sugar-beet fields, she chops
rattlesnake heads. She cannot
cast them far enough. Venom lips.
She dances in rags,
scabs flaking, her jesus heavy.
Icicles hang in her words. She is
a hunched bear with golden ears.

We are collectors,
each one of us
picking garbage,
hoarding our treasures.
I find a one-eyed doll,
smiling cracked face, a carriage
where I sit my new baby,
a rubber snake, a halloween spider,
a Chinese butterly.

âcimowinis

Ram Woman, we met for the first time.
You stood on top of graves at White Rabbit,
large eye staring.
My legs wrapped my husband.
Your head thumped those stones.

Ram Womam, I stood naked
beneath the falls.
Your hoofs pounded
in that April rain. I remember
your fist in your mother's womb,
heels kicking her door.
When her lips split
two birds flew
from your mouth. You
lifted your moccasins
in a Ghost Dance.
While the drummers sang
dogs ran after your meat
and bones, pissed at your feet.
You let them in. They left
nickels and dimes.

Ram Woman, always in pursuit
of the laughing sun,
the pregnant moon.
A gorging river, you plunge
heedless into the spring fire.
You drag your laughing, weeping
child in a trail of snares, shutting
out the wind.

Ram Woman, Ram Woman
in Kootenay Plains you sang,
lured me to your grave,
gave my heart a twist and
sent me flying, gave me
your large eye
for my stepping stone.

She came in a Vision, flipped many faces.
Stone-aged wrinkled, creased like a stretched drum,
thin flesh, sharp nose.
When the Sun sleeps she takes faded rays,
dresses her gown. She's the burnt rose of autumn,
a blue-winged warbler. The awakened river
flanked in every woman, rolling pebbles
over and over till stone eggs are left.
I travel with her youth, this Night Mistress.
Hair fresh, sweet grass braided in perfection.
Long ago Grandmother danced in glades,
women crushed chokecherries, saved the blood,
cleaned porcupine quills,
weaved them into birch baskets, chewed sinew.
They drummed, danced, lifted their dreams.
Ribboned the Sky.
Raw-boned,
they left their blood.
In these moccasin gardens
I pick my medicines.

I talk to Magpies. Their eyes my Womanhood.
How can I mark that?
The first ecstasy of climax?
Each squealing baby?
When told to cross my legs at ceremony?
When told never to walk over men when I was in

Full Moon?
Or was it the first time I gave away all my jeans,
sexy dresses and wore tents for a year?

Did our Grandmothers know we would be scarred
by the fists and boots of men?
Our songs taxed,
silenced by tongues that speak damnation and burning?
Did they know we would turn woman against woman?
Did they know some of us would follow,
take mates of colour and how the boarding of our worlds
would pulse breathing exiles connected to their womb?
Did they know only some would dig roots, few hands
calloused from tanning? Did they know only a few
would know the preparation of moose nose, gopher,
beaver-tail feasts? Did they know our memory, our
talk would walk on paper, legends told sparingly?
Did they know of our struggling hearts?

Each month Grandmother waxes and wanes,
pregnant with wolverine and baying dog.
I become heat at Midnight,
a yowling cat, fingers stained. Quills.
Mark these songs.

We are Star People.
wîsahkêcâhk sang to the Water People
to bring back Earth from where we dove.
She pinched the mud from the exhausted Muskrat.
Blew *yôtin*. Blew *iskotêw*. *iskwêw* was born.
pimâtisiwin fills woman.
Man is born.

I return to the Moon glade,
turn up the sod,
lift up my songs.

Dream.
Grandmother dances at Midnight.
Grandmother Moon,
my Shadow
dreams the dark.

Grandmother, the Woman in me.

A pagan. Again.

All my relations. *ahâw.*

Acknowledgements

My prayers and thanks to the Great Mystery and to the Spirit
Helpers, to All My Relations for the help bestowed on making
this work possible. To my great teacher, the late Elder, JP Cardinal;
may his teachings and his memory live; and to his wife Jenny,
thank you for your love and support throughout all my fledging
years. To my beloved who was there right from the day we set eyes
on one another, thank you for your love and your faith. A book is
never written alone, is never successful on its journey without its
readers, its friends, its critics, its editors and publishers, thank you
all for your laying of hands and seeing with your big heavens. I am
especially grateful to Coteau Books. They believed *Blue Marrow*
had merit. They believed it had a strong back and big wings.
Old JP Cardinal once said that of one of its characters. I was given
an opportunity to revisit the text in a new way, and I am deeply
appreciative of the vision that resulted from this. Thank you to my
adopted bro., Tim Lilburn, for his expert eye on the fine tuning.
Thank you to Jean Okimâsis and Arok Wolvengrey for their
wonderful work with the Cree language. *mîkwêc* for all of your
love, your support. *hâw!*

Cree Glossary

Prepared by Louise Halfe; edited and expanded by Jean Okimâsis and Arok Wolvengrey.

ahâw, all right, okay, that's it

amisk, beaver

asiniyak, rocks

asiskiy, 1. earth, 2. soil, 3. dirt, 4. clay, 5. mud

aski-pahkwêsikan, 1. flour, 2. bread, 3. "earth cut into bread," 4. raw bread

askipwâwa, 1. potatoes, 2. "earth eggs," 3. "eggs born of earth"

askiy, earth, soil

awâsis, child

ayamihâ, 1. pray, 2. give a difficult time to it in prayer

âcimo, tell stories, tell news

âcimostawinân, tell us stories

âcimowina, stories

âcimowinisa, small stories

âkayâsiwak, Englishmen

âmow-mêyi, 1. bee shit, 2. honey

âniskotâpânak, great, great grandparents

âsay, already

âstam, come, come here

âyimani-sîpiy, Difficult River

cahkipêhikana, Syllabics

câpân, Great Grandmother or Great Grandfather, it is not gender specific.

câpânak, Great Grandmothers or Great Grandfathers

ci-cîmân, Little Canoe

cihcipistikwân, Rolling Head

cistêmâw, tobacco

ê-kiskisiyâhk, we (exclusive) remember (i.e. we but not the person(s) spoken to)

ê-kî-âhtaskêyân, s/he puts her/his land elsewhere

ê-ma-môniyâskwêhkâsoyâhk, we are acting like white women

ê-mamâhtâwisit, she is gifted

ê-pêcimakik, with my wails they respond

ê-sôhkêpayik, it is powerful

êkwa, and

ihkwak, lice

iskotêw, fire

iskwêw, woman

iskwêwak, women

itâskonikêwin, the lifting of the Pipe

iyinimina, blueberries

kahkiyaw, all

kahkiyaw iskwêwak, all women

kahkiyaw nâpêwak, all men

kayâs-âcimowin, ancient story

kâ-itwêhât, Makes Him Talk

kâ-wî-nânapâcihikoyâhk, that which will heal us

kâhkêwak, 1. dried meat, 2. jerky

kâkîsimo, pray in a traditional manner

kiki-pîcicînânaw, we will dance the Round Dance

kikiskisin cî, do you remember?

kimaskihkîm, your medicine

kimiwan-piyêsîs, Raining Bird

kinwêsk, for a long time

kisêwâtisiwin, kindness

kisêyiniw-wâpiskiwiyâs, 1. the Old White Flesh, 2. an old whiteman

kisêyiniwak, the very Elderly Men; they are held in high esteem

kiskisiw, she remembers

kitaskînaw, our land

kitânisak, your daughters

kitimâkinawinân, take pity on us

kiwîcisânihtonâwâw, you are related (by blood) as siblings

kîsik, 1. sky, 2. the Heavens

kîwêtinohk, 1. Carrying the bundles home, 2. North

kôhkom, your grandmother

kwâhkotêw, it blazes

masânak, nettles, thistles

maskihkîwâpoy, 1. medicine tea, 2. Labrador tea

maskwacîs, Little Bear Hills; Hobbema, Alberta

matotisân, the Sweatlodge; the lodge where All Relations bear witness of tears and healing

mâmaw-ôhtâwîmâw, Creator of All, Giver of Life

mâmâ, my mom

mâmitonêyihtêstamâsowin, deliberate, weighing thought

mâto, cry

micihciya, hands

miskîsik, 1. eye, 2. "big heaven"

mistasinîwi-sîpiy, Big Stone River

mistikôsiwak, Frenchmen

mitâtaht, ten

miyohtâkwan, it sounds good

mîkwêc, thanks [Saulteaux word]

mînisa, berries

môhkomâna, knives

môniyaw-kisêyiniw, old whiteman

môniyâsak, the Whites

namôya ê-kaskihtâyân kîkway, I did not know anything

nâpêsisak, boys

nâpêwak, men

nicawâsimis, my child

nikamowak, they sing

nikamowinis, little song

nikâwiy, my mother

nimosôm, my grandfather

nimosômak, my grandfathers

nipiy, water

nipônênân, we add it to the fire, we make a fire

nipwâm, my thigh

nitânis, my daughter

nitânisak, my daughters

nîci, fellow, my friend

nîcimos, my sweetheart

nôhkom, my grandmother

nôhkom âtayôhkan, Grandmother Keeper of the Sacred Legends

nôhkomak, my grandmothers

nôsisim, my grandchild

nôsisimak, my grandchildren

nôtokwêsiw, old woman

nôtokwêsiwak, the very Elderly Women; they are held in high
    esteem

ohkomipan, the Eternal/Ethereal Grandmother

ohkomipanak, Eternal/Ethereal Grandmothers, Grandmothers of
    extreme depth

ohkwâkan, his/her face

okâwîmâwaskiy, 1. Mother Earth, 2. Beyond the Horizon Earth
    Mother, 3. the Infinite Earth Mother

okiniyak, rosehips

omikiya, scabs

omosômimâwak, grandfathers

omosômipanak, the Eternal/Ethereal Grandfathers

opîtatowêwak, 1. Ukrainians, 2. Europeans

oskana kâ-asastêki, 1. Bone-Pile-Up, 2. Where the Bones are Piled,
    3. Regina, Saskatchewan

oskîsik, his/her eye

ospwâkan, pipe

pahkisimotâhk, 1. where the Sun sets, 2. west

pawâkan, 1. Dream Spirit, 2. Guardian of Dreams and Visions

pâpâ, my dad

pâskisikana, guns

pâspâscês, Woodpecker

pê-nânapâcihinân, come heal us

pê-nîhtaciwêk, come down, climb downhill

pê-wâpan ôma, dawn has come

pimâtisi, live

pimâtisiwin, life

piyêsiwak, the Thunders

piyêsîs, bird

piyêsîsak, birds

pîcicî, dance the Round Dance

pîsim, Sun

sawêyiminân, bless us, cherish us

sâkihitowin, love

sîpi-kiskisiw, 1. she remembers far back, 2. long term memory, as in
    river memory or artesian memory

sîpîsis, creek

sîsîpaskihk, 1. kettle, 2. duck pail

sîwinikan, sugar

sôhkêciwani-sîpiy, Fast Flowing River, Strong Current River

sôhkêyimo, persevere, be brave

tawahikan, 1. the land/horizon of abundant beauty and life, 2. to
    clear a spot, make a space, make room for

wahotêw, a reed with edible root

waniskâ, arise, get up from bed

wâpâsôs, Early Riser

wâpikwaniya, 1. flowers, 2. dawn flowers

wâsatinaw, bright hill

wêpinâsowin, 1. something thrown in the wind, 2. a flower print, 3. material that flows in the wind, 4. an offering, 5. a flag

wîcisânihtowin, blood relation

wîhkês, rat root, a bitter medicinal root

wîhta, tell it

wîhtam, he/she tells it

wîhtikow, Cannibalistic Being

wîsahkêcâhk, Culture Hero, Trickster

yôtin, wind, it is windy

yôtin-nâpêsis, Windy Boy

PHOTO: DON DENTON

About the Author

Louise Bernice Halfe's first book of poetry, *Bear Bones &*
Feathers, won the Milton Acorn People's Poet award, and
was a finalist for the Spirit of Saskatchewan Award, the Pat
Lowther Award, and the Gerald Lampert Award. Her work
has appeared in various anthologies and magazines. *Blue*
Marrow was nominated for the Governor General's Award in
1998.

Louise Bernice Halfe, also known as Sky Dancer, was born
in Two Hills, Alberta. She was raised on the Saddle Lake
Indian Reserve and attended Blue Quills Residential School.
She has travelled extensively across Canada and abroad
doing readings and presentations of her work.